Content

How to Use This Book

Mathematical Thinking: Linking Math to Everyday Life enables second-grade learners to see a connection between the math concepts they learn in the classroom and their everyday experiences. As learners begin to understand the usefulness of the skills they are taught, they appreciate why these skills are necessary. *Mathematical Thinking: Linking Math to Everyday Life* is designed to help learners develop this appreciation and build a stronger foundation of integral mathematical concepts.

Mathematical Thinking: Linking Math to Everyday Life features six sections. Each section offers four curriculum-based activities, derived from standards set by the National Council of Teachers of Mathematics (NCTM). The activities involve important vocabulary, concepts, and skills taught in second-grade math classrooms across the United States. The activities also offer engaging fun facts related to the subject matter, easy-to-understand skill definitions, and simple directions for learners to follow. *Mathematical Thinking: Linking Math to Everyday Life* will help your learner master the math skills necessary for classroom success.

▣▶ Math in the Classroom
The first section of this book helps learners connect the math concepts they learn in school to various classroom situations. Since young learners spend much of their time in school, the classroom is a very familiar place. The activities involve geometry, word problems focusing on basic operations, and graphing.

▣▶ Math in the Kitchen
The second section of this book focuses on the many ways that classroom math skills can be applied in the kitchen. Learners implement these concepts by converting units of volume, working with recipes, measuring time for cooking, and counting calories. The activities in this section enable learners to have fun with the skills they are taught.

2

▣▷ Sports Math

The third section of this book engages learners by connecting math concepts to sports. Many learners exhibit great interest in this area, as it is often a big part of their lives. The activities in this section focus on demonstrating how classroom math skills are linked to physical education and team sports. Learners answer word problems, plot coordinate points, read a scoreboard, and perform basic operations.

▣▷ Family Math

The fourth section of this book involves demonstrating the various ways that math skills can be used in family situations. Learners practice applying math concepts such as map reading, scheduling, and completing word problems in circumstances related to family life.

▣▷ Math at the Store

The fifth section of this book explores the connection between classroom math and the grocery store. As learners practice making change, understanding weight, recognizing geometric shapes, and understanding food temperatures, they gain valuable insight into the numerous ways math can be used in a familiar store setting.

▣▷ Math at the Park

In the final section of this book, learners encounter activities set at the park. The activities continue to highlight the link between classroom math and real-world situations. Learners work with reflections, complete word problems, practice map reading, and read thermometers in these charming exercises.

Name _____

Classroom Word Problems

✏️▶ **Directions: Answer the questions below.**

1 There are 30 students in Ms. Sobbet's class. There are 16 boys. How many of Ms. Sobbet's students are girls? _____

2 Ms. Sobbet decides to arrange her students' desks in groups of 5. How many groups of 5 desks will there be? _____

3A Four new students join Ms. Sobbet's class. Three of them are girls. How many girls are there in Ms. Sobbet's class now? _____

B How many boys are there in Ms. Sobbet's class now? _____

4

Name _____

Cooking Time

> **Directions: Answer the questions below.**

1 Anna started cooking green beans at 🕐 . They must cook for 20 minutes. What time will the green beans be ready to eat?

_____

2 Eric started cooking macaroni at 🕐 . It must cook for 11 minutes. What time will the macaroni be ready to eat?

_____

3 Laura started cooking chili at 🕐 . It must cook for 55 minutes. What time will the chili be ready to eat?

_____

4 Steve started cooking rice at 🕐 . It must cook for 20 minutes. What time will the rice be ready to eat?

_____

Name _____

Gym Class

✏️ **Directions: Answer the questions below.**

1 Carlos did 25 sit-ups at the beginning of the year. Now he can do 11 more. How many sit-ups can Carlos do now?

_____

2 Charlie climbed the rope in 15 seconds at the beginning of the year. Now he can do it in 12 seconds. What is the difference in his climbing times?

_____

3 Lauren was able to make 10 baskets at the beginning of the year. Now she can make 8 more. How many baskets can Lauren make now?

_____

4 Greg did 36 jumping jacks at the beginning of the year. Now he can do 49 jumping jacks. How many more can he do now?

_____

6

Name _____

My Schedule

> ✏️ **Directions:** Think about the things you did today. Draw hands on the clocks below to show a certain time of day. Next to each clock, draw a picture of what you did at that time.

1

2

3

4

Name _____

Money at the Store

> ✏ **Directions: Use this chart to answer the questions below.**

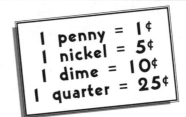

```
1 penny  =  1¢
1 nickel  =  5¢
1 dime  =  10¢
1 quarter  =  25¢
```

1A Julie's mom gives her $1.00 to buy a banana. If the banana costs 40¢, how much money does Julie have left?

_____

B In the space below, write down one combination of coins that equals the amount of money Julie has left.

_____

2A Alexander's brother gives him $1.50 to buy a magazine. If the magazine costs 75¢, how much money does Alexander have left?

_____

B In the space below, write down one combination of coins that equals the amount of money Alexander has left.

_____

Name _____

Picnic Word Problems

✏️➡️ **Directions: Use the information about Jill's family to answer the questions below.**

Jill's family is having a picnic at the park. Listed below are the family members that come to the picnic:

Jill	2 brothers	2 aunts
Mom	Grandma	5 male cousins
Dad	Grandpa	6 female
2 sisters	2 uncles	cousins

1 All of the female family members drink juice at the picnic. Everyone else drinks milk. How many people drink milk? _____

2 There are 4 picnic tables at the park. If an equal number of people sit at each table, how many of Jill's family members will sit at each table? _____

3 Jill, her mom, all of her cousins, one uncle, and both aunts decide to take a walk around the lake. How may people walk around the lake? _____

Teaching Tips...

TEACHING TIPS

- **Background**

  As learners acquire number concepts and skills, it is important to link these skills to familiar surroundings, such as the classroom. In this section, learners develop their understanding of basic operations, fractions, geometry, and graphing while completing activities based on classroom situations.

- **Homework Helper**

  After completing the Geometry in the Classroom activity on page 12, have learners draw five geometric shapes on a piece of paper. Next, have learners locate and list objects at home that are similar to those five shapes.

- **Research-based Activity**

  After learners complete the Graphing Class Information activity on page 14, have them survey their classmates on a topic of their choice (eye color, hair color, sport preference, favorite holiday, etc.). After the data has been collected, have learners construct bar graphs to display what they have discovered about their classmates.

- **Test Prep**

  Graphing is a skill necessary in many classroom activities. As a result, standardized tests often feature graphs in sections on social studies and science. By becoming familiar with graphs, learners will achieve success in these sections, as well as those based on math.

- **Different Audiences**

  If you are working with an accelerated learner, try introducing other types of graphs, such as pie graphs and pictographs. Explain to the learner that there are multiple ways to visually display information. Have learners use one set of data to create three different kinds of graphs.

Name _____

Classroom Word Problems

We can add, subtract, multiply, and divide to solve word problems about the students in our class.

Example: *Mr. Dean has 25 pencils and 5 students. If he gives each student an equal number of pencils, how many pencils does each student get? Answer: 25 ÷ 5 = 5*

➡ **Directions: Answer the following questions about Mr. Dean's second-grade class.**

1 There are 32 students in Mr. Dean's class. There are 16 girls. How many of Mr. Dean's students are boys?   _____

2 Mr. Dean rearranges the students' desks into groups. Each group has 4 desks. If there are 32 students in his class, how many groups of 4 desks are there?   _____

3 Mr. Dean orders pizza for his class for lunch. He orders enough pizza for each of his 32 students to have one slice each. If there are 8 slices of pizza in a pie, how many pizza pies does Mr. Dean order?   _____

4 Three new students join Mr. Dean's class of 32 students. Two students leave the class. How many students are in Mr. Dean's class now?   _____

Name _____

Geometry in the Classroom

We can find geometric shapes in the classroom by knowing what to look for.

Example*: We know that a cone looks like this:*
We can find cones in the real world, such as this ice cream cone:

Directions: Look at the shapes below. Next to each shape, list a classroom object that looks like that shape.

1

Rectangle

2

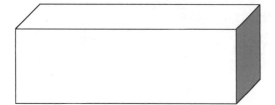

Rectangular Prism

Today, a school is made up of many classrooms. In the past, children of all ages learned together in one room.

Classroom Word Problems

We can use fractions to solve word problems about things that happen at school.

Example: *There are 10 teachers at a school. Three of them leave to work at another school. What fraction of the teachers are left?*

Answer: $\frac{10}{10} - \frac{3}{10} = \frac{7}{10}$ $\qquad$ $\frac{7}{10}$ of the teachers are left.

▭▷ **Directions: Answer the following questions.**

1 Nick has 9 pencils. He offers Annie 2 of them. What fraction of the 9 pencils does Nick have left?

_____

2 Aaron has 4 crayons. Francesca has 5 crayons. Aaron offers Francesca $\frac{1}{2}$ of his crayons. How many crayons does Francesca have now?

_____

3 The teacher asks Erica and Matt to hand out worksheets to the class. There are 20 students in the class. If the teacher gives $\frac{1}{2}$ of the worksheets to Erica and $\frac{1}{2}$ to Matt, how many worksheets will each of them hand out?

_____

Name _____

Graphing Class Information

We can make graphs to help us organize information about our lives.

Directions: Mrs. Leary has asked her students to choose classroom jobs. Make a bar graph that shows how many students would like each job.

10 students want to collect papers

4 students want to hand out papers

6 students want to keep the bookshelf neat

5 students want to keep the art supplies neat

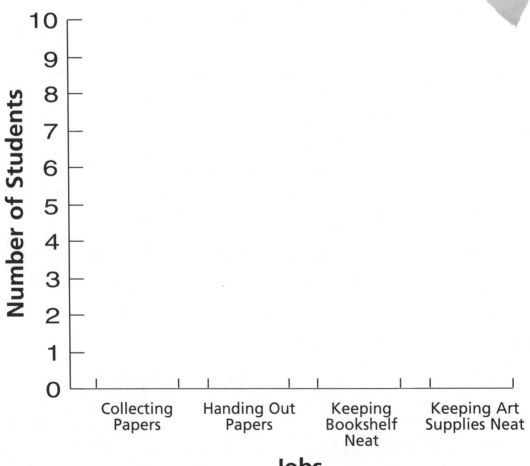

Name _____

Skill Check—Math in the Classroom

Classroom Word Problems and Graphing Class Information

1 Mrs. Carmen has 24 students in her class. If 13 of them are girls, how many are boys? _____

2 On a separate sheet of paper, make a bar graph showing the number of girls and boys in Mrs. Carmen's class.

Geometry in the Classroom

Directions: Write the name of the shape that each classroom object looks like in the space provided.

1 _____   2 _____   3 _____

15

• Background

Because food plays a central role in everyday life, it is important for learners to recognize the integral role that math plays in the kitchen. In this section, learners develop an understanding of this role as they determine units of volume, measure time and ingredients for cooking, and learn to count calories of different foods.

• Homework Helper

Ask learners to select five items that are in their original packaging from their kitchens at home. Have learners study each package to find the weight of each item in ounces. Next, have learners list these items from heaviest to lightest. Learners can compare their lists to see the different weights at which foods are packaged and sold.

• Research-based Activity

After completing the Recipes and Measurement activity on page 18, have learners look through a cookbook and select a recipe they find interesting. Ask them to cut that recipe in half and list the new amounts of each ingredient.

• Test Prep

Understanding the relationship between math concepts and their many applications in the kitchen will prepare learners for classroom testing. As they recognize the reasons why skills are introduced to them, learners build a stronger foundation for success on these tests.

• Different Audiences

Present a learner for whom English is a second language (ESL) with food items in various types of packages. Explain how to read the different labels to learn about caloric content and package weight using the English system of measurement. Offer these learners a worksheet with conversions between the metric and English systems.

16

Name _____

Units of Volume

Volume is a measurement of how much a container can hold. We can use the units of ounces, cups, pints, quarts, and gallons to measure the volume of different foods.
Example: *1 cup = 8 ounces*

May drank 3 cups of water. How many ounces of water did she drink? Answer: 3 x 8 ounces = 24 ounces

Directions: Use the chart to answer the questions below.

8 OUNCES = 1 CUP
2 CUPS = 1 PINT
2 PINTS = 1 QUART
4 QUARTS = 1 GALLON

1 Julie drank 2 cups of juice with her breakfast. How many ounces of juice did she drink?

_____

2 Sam poured 3 quarts of milk into a pot. How many pints of milk did he pour?

_____

3 Kyle has 8 quarts of apple cider. How many gallons of apple cider does he have?

_____

Name _____

Recipes and Measurement

Recipes list specific measurements of ingredients. By combining just the right amount of ingredients, we can make different foods.

Carlos and his mother want to bake a small batch of cookies. Help them cut their recipe in half.

Example: *If the original recipe calls for 1 cup of flour, Carlos should use half of that amount, or $\frac{1}{2}$ cup of flour.*

Directions: Finish each statement below by finding one half of the measurement given.

1 If the original recipe calls for 2 cups of sugar, Carlos

should use _____ cup.

2 If the original recipe calls for 4 eggs, Carlos should use

_____ eggs.

3 If the original recipe calls for 8 tablespoons of butter,

Carlos should use _____ tablespoons.

FUN FACT

Chocolate chip cookies are the most popular cookies in the United States of America.

Name _____

Recipes and Time

Recipes list specific amounts of time to cook food. To measure that amount of time, we use a clock when we begin. Then we add the amount of time listed in the recipe to the time on the clock to figure out what time the food will be ready.

Example: *If Melanie started cooking a chicken at* 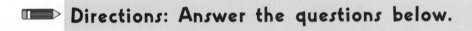 *, and it must cook for 30 minutes, what time will it be ready to eat? Answer: 6:15 + 30 minutes = 6:45*

Directions: Answer the questions below.

1 Jill started cooking pasta at ⏰. It must cook for 10 minutes. What time will it be ready to eat?_____

2 Ben started cooking broccoli at ⏰. It must cook for 20 minutes. What time will it be ready to eat?_____

3 Michele started cooking potatoes at ⏰. They must cook for 30 minutes. What time will they be ready to eat?_____

Undercooked describes food that has not been cooked long enough. **Overcooked** describes food that has been cooked for too long.

19

Name _____

Counting Calories

A calorie is a measure of how much energy food can supply your body. All foods have calories. When you eat, your body uses the food as fuel, burning it to produce energy.
Example: *We can count the calories we eat to make sure our bodies have enough energy. If you eat an 81-calorie apple and drink a 120-calorie glass of milk, how many calories have you eaten? Answer: 120 calories + 81 calories = 201 calories*

➡ **Directions: Use the menu to answer the questions below.**

MENU

Pizza	450 calories	Apple	81 calories
Chicken Nuggets	350 calories	Pear	110 calories
Cheese Sandwich	250 calories	Cookie	65 calories
Juice	130 calories	Milk	120 calories
Soda	140 calories	Chocolate Milk	180 calories

1 It is lunchtime in the school cafeteria. Ella chooses pizza, a pear, and juice for lunch. How many calories does she eat?_____

2 Jeremy chooses a cheese sandwich, a cookie, and chocolate milk for lunch. How many calories does he eat?_____

3 Alvin chooses chicken nuggets, soda, and an apple for lunch. How many calories does he eat?_____

 FUN FACT

A healthy diet includes calories from protein, carbohydrates, and healthy fats.

Name _____

Skill Check—Math in the Kitchen

Units of Volume

1 How many cups are equal to 6 pints? _____

2 How many quarts are equal to 2 gallons? _____

Recipes and Measurement

🖊 **Directions: Find one half of each measurement in the recipe given.**

1 4 cups of flour _____

2 6 eggs _____

Recipes and Time

1 Andrew started cooking fish at 🕖. It needs to cook for 18 minutes. What time will the fish be ready to eat?

_____

2 Jamie started baking a cake at 🕐. It needs to bake for 45 minutes. What time will the cake be ready to eat?

_____

TEACHING TIPS

- **Background**

  Math concepts and sports are closely linked. From physical education classes to team sports, the opportunities to link math concepts to the real world abound. Since many learners are involved with or interested in sports, they will respond positively to these connections, furthering their understanding of the skills they are taught.

- **Homework Helper**

  Have learners watch part of a sporting event, such as a baseball or basketball game. Ask them to list any parts of the game they can identify that use familiar math concepts.

- **Research-based Activity**

  Ask learners to search the Internet to find out how many players there are on different types of sports teams. Have them make a chart or graph to show their results. Discuss how scoreboards are types of charts used to show a game's data.

- **Test Prep**

  The activities in this section cover many math concepts that appear on standardized and classroom tests, such as basic operations, plotting ordered pairs, and reading a chart. As learners complete the activities, they practice working with these skills.

- **Different Audiences**

  Have an accelerated learner create number sentences using <, >, and = to show comparisons between different professional baseball teams' scores. You can provide the learner with a list of scores or have the learner look them up on the Internet.

Name _____

Gym Class

We can use math to see how our physical fitness improves in gym class.
Example: *It took Laura 20 seconds to climb the rope in the beginning of the year. After practicing, she was able to climb the rope in 16 seconds. What is the difference in her climbing times? Answer: 20 seconds − 16 seconds = 4 seconds*

Directions: Answer the questions below.

1 Molly did 40 jumping jacks at the beginning of the year. Now she can do 60 jumping jacks. How many more can she do now?

_____

2 Nancy did 33 sit-ups in the beginning of the year. Now she can do 45 sit-ups. How many more can she do now?

_____

3 Eleanor was able to make 14 baskets at the beginning of the year. Now she can make 13 more. How many baskets can she make now?

_____

FUN FACT

Exercising is a great way to keep your body healthy!

23

Name _____

Team Sports

Team coaches often use grids to show their team players where to stand on the field.

Example: This grid shows where one coach wants his players to stand on a part of a field.

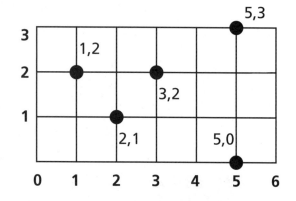

Directions: Plot the coordinates given on the grid below to help Coach Nielsen show his players where to stand. Label each point with that player's letter.

Player A (1, 3)

Player B (5, 2)

Player C (4, 1)

Player D (3, 1)

Player E (7, 5)

Player F (3, 8)

Name _____

Reading a Scoreboard

We can read a scoreboard to find out information about a game.

	Innings		
	1st	2nd	3rd
Tigers	0	2	0
Bears	1	1	1

Example: *Which team won the game? Tigers score = 0+2+0 = 2*
Bears score = 1+1+1 = 3   2< 3, therefore the Bears won the game.

Directions: Use the scoreboard to help you answer the questions below.

	Innings						
	1st	2nd	3rd	4th	5th	6th	7th
Blues	2	3	0	0	1	0	1
Reds	1	1	4	1	0	2	0

1 How many runs did the Reds score in the 5th inning? _____

2 How many runs did the Blues score in the first 3 innings? _____

3 Which team won the game? _____

The National Baseball Hall of Fame & Museum is located in Cooperstown, N.Y. It was created in 1935 to celebrate baseball's 100th anniversary.

Name _____

Sports Equipment

Ms. Kana is going to order new equipment for her gym class. She is allowed to order:

3 basketballs for every 10 students
1 jump rope for every 3 students
2 plastic bats for every 5 students
2 kick balls for every 6 students

Directions: There are 30 students in Ms. Kana's class. Use the chart above to figure out how many of the following items she can order.

1 Basketballs _____

2 Jump ropes _____

3 Plastic bats _____

4 Kick balls _____

FUN FACT

The Women's National Basketball Association played their first season in 1997.

Name _____

Skill Check–Sports Math

Gym Class

1 Kelly climbed the rope in 34 seconds at the beginning of the year. Now she can do it in 29 seconds. What is the difference in her climbing times?

2 Mark did 25 sit-ups at the beginning of the year. Now he can do 12 more. How many sit-ups can Mark do now?

_____

_____

Team Sports

✏️➤ **Directions: Plot the coordinates given to help Coach Nikita show her players where to stand on the field.**

Player A (3, 2)

Player B (4, 1)

Player C (2, 5)

Player D (5, 4)

Player E (1, 3)

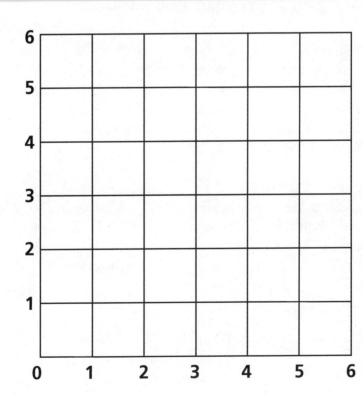

- ## Background

  In this section, learners encounter several key math concepts, presented in activities related to family situations. Learners practice reading a map, creating a schedule, and answering word problems that require them to perform basic operations.

- ## Homework Helper

  After completing the My Schedule activity on page 30, have learners create a schedule to follow over a weekend. Have them choose four activities for each day, such as cleaning their rooms or helping cook a meal with a parent. Provide learners with a worksheet with eight blank clocks on which they can draw hands to represent the times they completed each activity.

- ## Research-based Activity

  After completing the Family Events Word Problems activity on page 31, have learners interview their relatives to find out the year in which each one was born. After they have collected this information, ask the learners to write equations to show how old each relative is.

- ## Test Prep

  All of the skills covered in this section provide learners with a strong foundation in organization. Map reading, scheduling, and collecting information in word problems are all concepts that teach learners to focus on organizing and selecting important information to answer questions. This skill is regularly evaluated in standardized testing.

- ## Different Audiences

  Help a challenged learner read an analog clock by providing him or her with a small digital clock to carry around. Periodically ask the learner to read an analog clock. After reading the analog clock, have the learner check his or her answer by reading the digital clock.

Name _____

Family Vacation

We can use a map to measure the distance a family travels on vacation.
Example: *The Kay family is going on vacation. How many miles will they travel from their home to the beach? Answer: 65 miles*

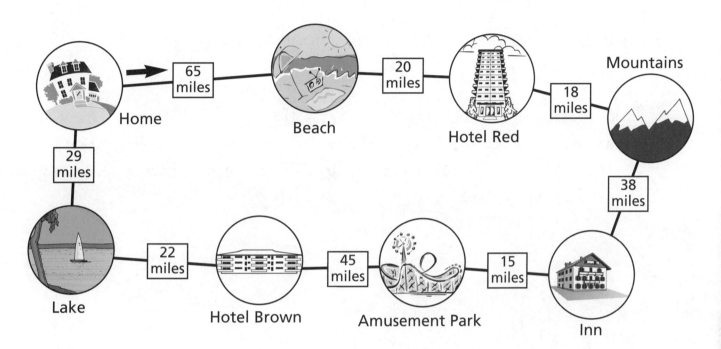

1 On Monday, the Kay family started at home and drove past the beach and Hotel Red to the mountains. How many miles did they drive that day?

_____

2 On Tuesday, the Kay family left the mountains and drove to the Inn. Then, they drove to the amusement park. How many miles did they drive that day?

_____

3 On Wednesday, the Kay family drove from the amusement park past Hotel Brown and the lake to their home. How many miles did they drive that day?

_____

29

Name _____

My Schedule

We use clocks to tell time. We keep track of the time so we are not late for things, such as school or dinner with our families.

Example: At , I wake up for school. I wake up at 7:15.

> ✏ **Directions:** Think about the activities you did today. Draw hands on each of the clocks below to show a certain time of day. Next to each clock, draw a picture of what you did at that time today.

1

2

3

 There are two types of clocks: analog and digital.

30

Name _____

Family Events Word Problems

We can use math to talk about when things happened in our lives. We can add and subtract to solve real-life word problems.
Example*: Barbara was born in 1995. If it is the year 2004, how old is Barbara? Answer: 2004 – 1995 = 9. Barbara is 9 years old.*

Directions: Answer the questions below.

1 Molly was born in 1990. If the year is 2004, how old is Molly?

_____

2 Alan and Kayla got married in 2001. Kayla was 30 years old at her wedding. What year was Kayla born?

_____

3 Debra's family moved to New Jersey in 1999. If the year is 2004, how many years has Debra's family lived in New Jersey?

_____

4 Todd's younger brother was born in 2000. Todd was four years old when his younger brother was born. If the year is 2004, how old is Todd?

_____

FUN FACT A family tree is a diagram that shows how all of the relatives in a family are connected.

31

Name _____

Family Garden Word Problems

We can use math to solve real-world word problems.

Example: *The Ross family is planting a garden in their yard. The garden is 32 square feet. There are 8 children in their family. If Mrs. Ross divides the garden up into 8 equal parts, how many square feet does each child get? Answer: 32 ÷ 8 = 4*

Directions: Answer the questions below.

1 Katie decides to plant 4 rows of tomato plants with 8 plants in each row. How many tomato plants will Katie have in all?

   _____

2 Meg plants 40 cucumber plants in the garden. She plants 5 equal rows of them. How many cucumber plants does Meg plant in each row?

   _____

3 Each of the 8 Ross children plants 5 broccoli plants and 2 spinach plants. How many broccoli and spinach plants are there in the garden?

   _____

4 Aly plants 3 times as many pepper plants as Jen does. If Jen plants 15 of them, how many pepper plants does Aly plant?

   _____

Name _____

Skill Check—Family Math

My Schedule

✏️ **Directions:** Draw hands on the clock to show a certain time of day. Next to it, draw a picture of something you would do at that time.

Family Events Word Problems

1 Evelyn was born in 1989. If the year is 2004, how old is Evelyn?

_____

2 Penny moved to Delaware when she was 18 years old. She lived there for 12 years. How old was Penny when she left Delaware?

_____

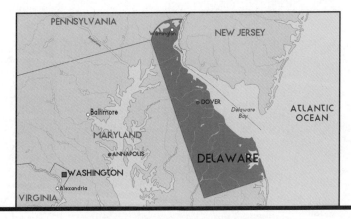

33

Teaching Tips...

TEACHING TIPS

- ## Background
  The skills covered in this section will help learners build confidence as conscientious consumers. Buying food in a grocery store requires knowledge of a variety of concepts. In the following activities, learners practice working with coins, performing basic operations, recognizing shapes, and recognizing the role temperature plays in keeping food fresh.

- ## Homework Helper
  Have learners find four food items that cost less than $1.00 each. Have them subtract the price of each of their items from $1.00 to see how much change they would receive from a cashier after paying for each with a dollar bill.

- ## Research-based Activity
  Have learners search the Internet to find prices of several items they have interest in buying, such as books, video games, or CDs. Ask learners to pretend that they can each spend $100 on these items. Have them add up the prices of their chosen items to see if they can afford to buy them.

- ## Test Prep
  Basic operation skills are frequently evaluated on class tests. The following activities provide ample practice in this area, helping learners build confidence in manipulating numbers.

- ## Different Audiences
  The practical applications of math concepts and grocery store vocabulary in this section can be very helpful to learners for whom English is a second language (ESL). Have these learners draw and label store items so they become more comfortable using the language.

34

Name _____

Money at the Store

We use math while shopping in a store. We can use math to pay for items with the right combination of dollars and coins.

Example: *Meg pays for a banana with 3 quarters. If the banana costs 70¢, how much money will Meg have left?*
Answer: 3 quarters = 75¢   75¢ – 70¢ = 5¢

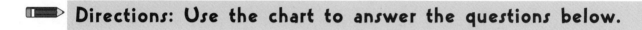

Directions: Use the chart to answer the questions below.

1A Amanda's uncle gives her $1.00 to buy an apple. If the apple costs 26¢, how much money will Amanda have left?

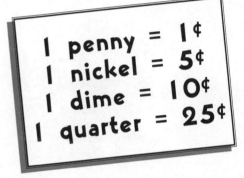

1 penny = 1¢
1 nickel = 5¢
1 dime = 10¢
1 quarter = 25¢

_____

B In the space below, write down one combination of coins that equal the amount of money Amanda has left.

_____

2A Corey's sister gives him $2.00 to buy a bottle of juice. The juice costs 78¢. How much money does Corey have left?

_____

B In the space below, write down one combination of coins that equal the amount of money Corey has left.

_____

Name _____

Food Weight and Number Sentences

The paper bags at the grocery store checkout counter will only hold up to 100 ounces (oz). If the weight of the groceries inside the bag is more than this amount, the bag will break.

Example: *12 oz + 10 oz + 35 oz $\boxed{<}$ 100 oz*

12 oz + 10 oz + 35 oz = 57 oz   Answer: 57 oz $\boxed{<}$ 100 oz

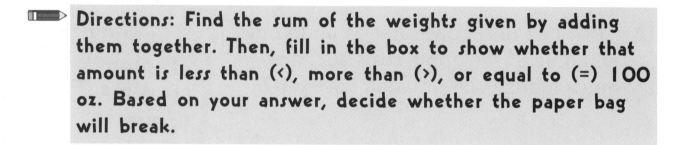

Directions: Find the sum of the weights given by adding them together. Then, fill in the box to show whether that amount is less than (<), more than (>), or equal to (=) 100 oz. Based on your answer, decide whether the paper bag will break.

1A 24 oz + 13 oz + 32 oz + 31 oz $\Box$ 100 oz

   B Will the bag break?_____

2A 71 oz + 28 oz + 1 oz $\Box$ 100 oz

   B Will the bag break?_____

3A 68 oz + 20 oz + 6 oz $\Box$ 100 oz

   B Will the bag break?_____

Some grocery stores will give you a few cents if you return your paper grocery bags to be used again.

Name _____

Geometry at the Store

Many geometric shapes can be found at the grocery store.
Examples: *A tissue box looks like a rectangular prism.*

A slice of pizza looks like a triangle.

✏️ **Directions: List two items you might find at the grocery store that match the shapes shown below.**

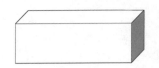

1A_____

B_____

rectangular prism

2A_____

B_____

cylinder

3A_____

B_____

sphere

Geometry is everywhere! Next time you eat a meal, see how many geometric shapes you can find on the table.

37

Name _____

Food Temperatures

Temperature plays an important part in keeping foods fresh at the grocery store. Some foods need to stay in a refrigerator, other foods need to stay in a freezer, and other foods can stay on shelves at room temperature.
Example: *Yogurt must stay in the refrigerator.*

Directions: Write the names of the foods that should be in the refrigerator under the word *refrigerator*. Next, write the names of the foods that should be in the freezer under the word *freezer*. Then, write the names of the foods that can stay on a shelf under the word *shelves*.

Tuna Fish   Ice Cream   Cheese   Cereal   Pretzels   Bread   Eggs

Refrigerator	Freezer	Shelves
_____	_____	_____
_____	_____	_____
_____	_____	_____

 **FUN FACT** Refrigerators were not used as home appliances until the 1930s.

Name _____

Skill Check—Math at the Store

Money

Alan's mom gives him $4.00 to buy milk and eggs. The milk costs $1.25. The eggs cost $2.50. How much money does Alan have left after buying these items?

_____

Food Weight

Directions: Find the sum of the weights below by adding them together. Fill in the box with <, >, or = to show the sum's relationship to 100 oz. Then answer the question.

1 14 oz + 18 oz + 24 oz + 5 oz ⬜ 100 oz

2 If the items inside the bag weigh more than 100 oz, the bag will break. Will the bag break?

_____

39

Teaching Tips...

For *Math at the Park*
(pp. 41–45)

- **Background**

  The activities in this section offer learners practice in geometry, basic operations, reading a map, and reading a thermometer. Each one links a math concept to the park, a situation that is very familiar to young learners.

- **Homework Helper**

  After completing the Reflections activity on page 41, give learners a worksheet with half of the human body on it. Explain how the body is symmetrical and have learners draw the other half.

- **Research-based Activity**

  Have learners do Internet research to learn how mirrors work. Ask them to write a paragraph about what they discover.

- **Test Prep**

  Providing learners with a familiar setting, such as a park, helps them feel comfortable in completing the following activities. The more comfortable learners feel, the more easily they will master this section's concepts, all of which appear on classroom tests.

- **Different Audiences**

  Help a challenged learner master reading a map by providing him or her with a simple one, such as of a school or a small town. Tour the area the map represents, allowing the challenged learner to use it to guide you. Have the learner show you how to get from one place to another on the map. Then, have him or her actually lead you to that place.

TEACHING TIPS

40

Name _____

Reflections

A reflection is an image produced on a shiny surface, such as a mirror or a body of water. If you look into a lake at the park, you will see your reflection.

Example:

This is a reflection of a semicircle.

> ✏️ **Directions: Look at the shapes below. Imagine each shape is at the edge of a lake. Draw the reflection of each shape in the lake.**

1

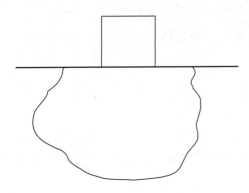

2

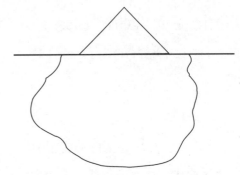

3

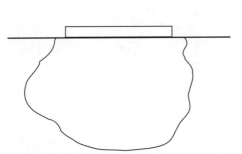

4

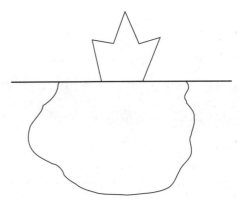

Name _____

Picnic Word Problems

We can use math to solve real-world word problems.

Michelle and her family go to the park for a picnic. Listed below are the family members that go to the park.

Michelle	**2 brothers**	**2 grandpas**	**6 female cousins**
Mom	**2 sisters**	**2 grandmas**	**3 male cousins**
Dad	**2 uncles**	**2 aunts**	

Directions: Use the information given above to answer the following questions.

1 All of the male family members decide to eat hot dogs at the picnic. Everyone else eats a hamburger. How many people eat hamburgers?

_____

2 There are 6 picnic tables in the picnic area. If an equal number of people sit at each table, how many of Michelle's family members sit at each table?

_____

3 One third of the family eats brownies for dessert. How many people eat brownies?

_____

There is a town named Picnic in Florida.

Name _____

Reading Maps at the Zoo

We can use maps to help us find our way.

> ✏️ **Directions: Use the map to answer the questions below.**

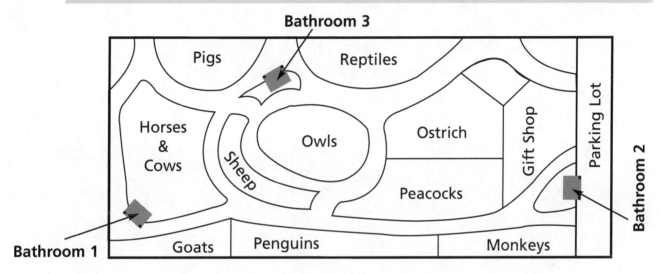

1 Are the owls or the peacocks closer to the pigs?

_____

2 Ari needs to go to the bathroom to wash his hands. He and his mother are looking at the goats. Which bathroom is closest to them?

_____

3 It is time for Ari and his mother to go home. Ari's mother says they can see one more animal before they go to the parking lot. Which animals are closest to the parking lot?

_____

Name _____

Temperature and Weather

We can read a thermometer to learn the temperature outside. The temperature tells us what it will feel like outside.
Example*: This thermometer reads 30° Farenheit (F). It will feel very cold outside.*

Directions: Draw a line from each thermometer to the picture that shows what the park might look like at that temperature.

1 **2** **3**

The first sealed thermometer, like the ones we use today, was invented by the German physicist Daniel Gabriel Fahrenheit in 1714.

44

Name _____

Skill Check—Math at the Park

Reflections

> ✏️ **Directions: Draw the reflections of the shapes below.**

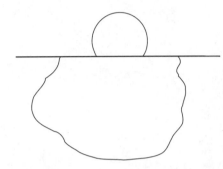 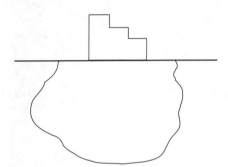

Family Picnic

1 The Moss family had a picnic in the park today. There were 32 family members in all. If 13 of them are women, how many members of the Moss family are men?

_____

2 There are 8 picnic tables at the park. If an equal number of people sit at each table, how many members of the Moss family sit at each table?

_____

Answer Key

p. 4
1) 14
2) 6
3A) 17
 B) 17

p. 5
1) 6:45
2) 4:26
3) 3:35
4) 8:30

p. 6
1) 36
2) 3 seconds
3) 18
4) 13

p. 7
Answers will vary.

p. 8
1A) 60¢
 B) Answers will vary.
2A) 75¢
 B) Answers will vary.

p. 9
1) 11
2) 6
3) 16

p. 11
1) 16
2) 8
3) 4
4) 33

p. 12
Answers will vary.

p. 13
1) $\frac{7}{9}$
2) 7
3) 10

p. 14

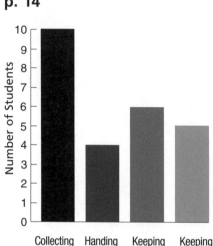

p. 15
**Classroom Word Problems
and Graphing Classroom
Information**
1) 11
2)

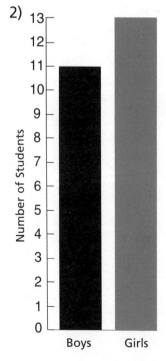

Geometry in the Classroom
1) sphere
2) rectangle
3) rectangular prism

p. 17
1) 16
2) 6
3) 2

p. 18
1) 1
2) 2
3) 4

p. 19
1) 6:00
2) 6:20
3) 6:15

p. 20
1) 690
2) 495
3) 571

p. 21
Units of Volume
1) 12
2) 8

Recipes and Measurement
1) 2 cups
2) 3 eggs

Recipes and Time
1) 4:48
2) 1:50

p. 23
1) 20
2) 12
3) 27

p. 24

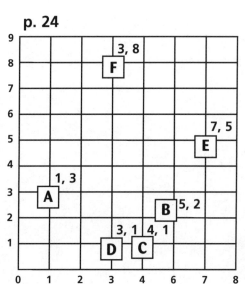

p. 25
1) 0
2) 5
3) Reds, 9-7

p. 26
1) 9
2) 10
3) 12
4) 10

p. 27
Gym Class
1) 5 seconds
2) 37

Team Sports

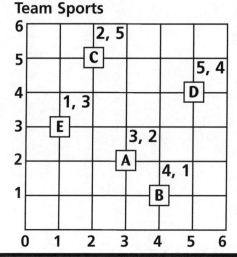

p. 29
1) 103
2) 53
3) 96

p. 30
Answers will vary.

p. 31
1) 14
2) 1971
3) 5
4) 8

p. 32
1) 32
2) 8
3) 56
4) 45

p. 33
My Schedule
Answers will vary.

Family Events
Word Problems
1) 15
2) 30

p. 35
1A) 74¢
  B) Answers will vary.
2A) $1.22
  B) Answers will vary.

p. 36
1A) =
  B) no
2A) =
  B) no
3A) <
  B) no

p. 37
Answers will vary.

p. 38
The cheese and eggs should be listed under *refrigerator*. The ice cream should be listed under *freezer*. The can of tuna fish, box of cereal, bag of pretzels, and loaf of bread should be listed under *shelf*.

p. 39
Money
25¢

Food Weight
1) <
2) no

p. 41

1   2

3   4

p. 42
1) 14
2) 4
3) 8

p. 43
1) owls
2) Bathroom 1
3) monkeys

p. 44
1) connected to winter scene
2) connected to fall scene
3) connected to summer scene

p. 45
Reflections

Family Picnic
1) 19
2) 4